I0836475

Published in New Orleans, Louisiana by JenVa Publishing

After this manner therefore pray ye: Our Father

which art in heaven, Hallowed be thy name.

Thy kingdom come, Thy will be done in earth, as it

is in heaven.

Give us this day our daily bread.

And forgive us our debts, as we forgive our debtors.

And lead us not into temptation, but deliver us from

MY PRAYER JOURNAL

Thank You

Thank Yo

MY PRAYER JOURNAL

Thank You

MY PRAYER JOURNAL

Thank You

MY PRAYER JOURNAL

MY PRAYER JOURNAL

Thank You

MY PRAYER JOURNAL

MY PRAYER JOURNAL

Thank You

MY PRAYER JOURNAL

Thank You

MY PRAYER JOURNAL

THANK YOU LORD

FOR

Ask, and it shall be given you; seek, and ye shall

find; knock, and it shall be opened unto you:

For every one that asketh receiveth; and he that

seeketh findeth; and to him that knocketh it shall

be opened.

Matthew 7:7-8

Thank You

MY PRAYER JOURNAL

MY PRAYER JOURNAL

Thank You

MY PRAYER JOURNAL

Thank You

MY PRAYER JOURNAL

MY PRAYER JOURNAL

Thank You

MY PRAYER JOURNAL

THANK YOU LORD

FOR

Be careful for nothing; but in everything by

prayer and supplication with thanksgiving let

your requests be made known unto God.

And the peace of God, which passeth all

understanding, shall keep your hearts and minds

through Christ Jesus.

Philippians 4:6-7

MY PRAYER JOURNAL

Thank You

MY PRAYER JOURNAL

MY PRAYER JOURNAL

Thank You

MY PRAYER JOURNAL

MY PRAYER JOURNAL

Thank You

MY PRAYER JOURNAL

Thank You

MY PRAYER JOURNAL

Thank You

THANK YOU LORD

FOR

Therefore I say unto you, What things soever ye
desire, when ye pray, believe that ye receive
them, and ye shall have them.
Mark 11:24

MY PRAYER JOURNAL

Thank You

MY PRAYER JOURNAL

MY PRAYER JOURNAL

Thank You

MY PRAYER JOURNAL

Thank You

MY PRAYER JOURNAL

Thank You

MY PRAYER JOURNAL

MY PRAYER JOURNAL

Thank You

THANK YOU LORD

FOR

Pray without ceasing.

I Thessalonians 5:17

MY PRAYER JOURNAL

MY PRAYER JOURNAL

Thank You

MY PRAYER JOURNAL

MY PRAYER JOURNAL

Thank You

MY PRAYER JOURNAL

Thank You

MY PRAYER JOURNAL

MY PRAYER JOURNAL

Thank You

Thank You

THANK YOU LORD

FOR

Likewise the Spirit also helpeth our infirmities:
for we know not what we should pray for as we
ought: but the Spirit itself maketh intercession
for us with groanings which cannot be uttered.
Romans 8:26

MY PRAYER JOURNAL

Thank You

MY PRAYER JOURNAL

Thank You

Thank You

MY PRAYER JOURNAL

MY PRAYER JOURNAL

Thank You

MY PRAYER JOURNAL

Thank You

THANK YOU LORD

FOR

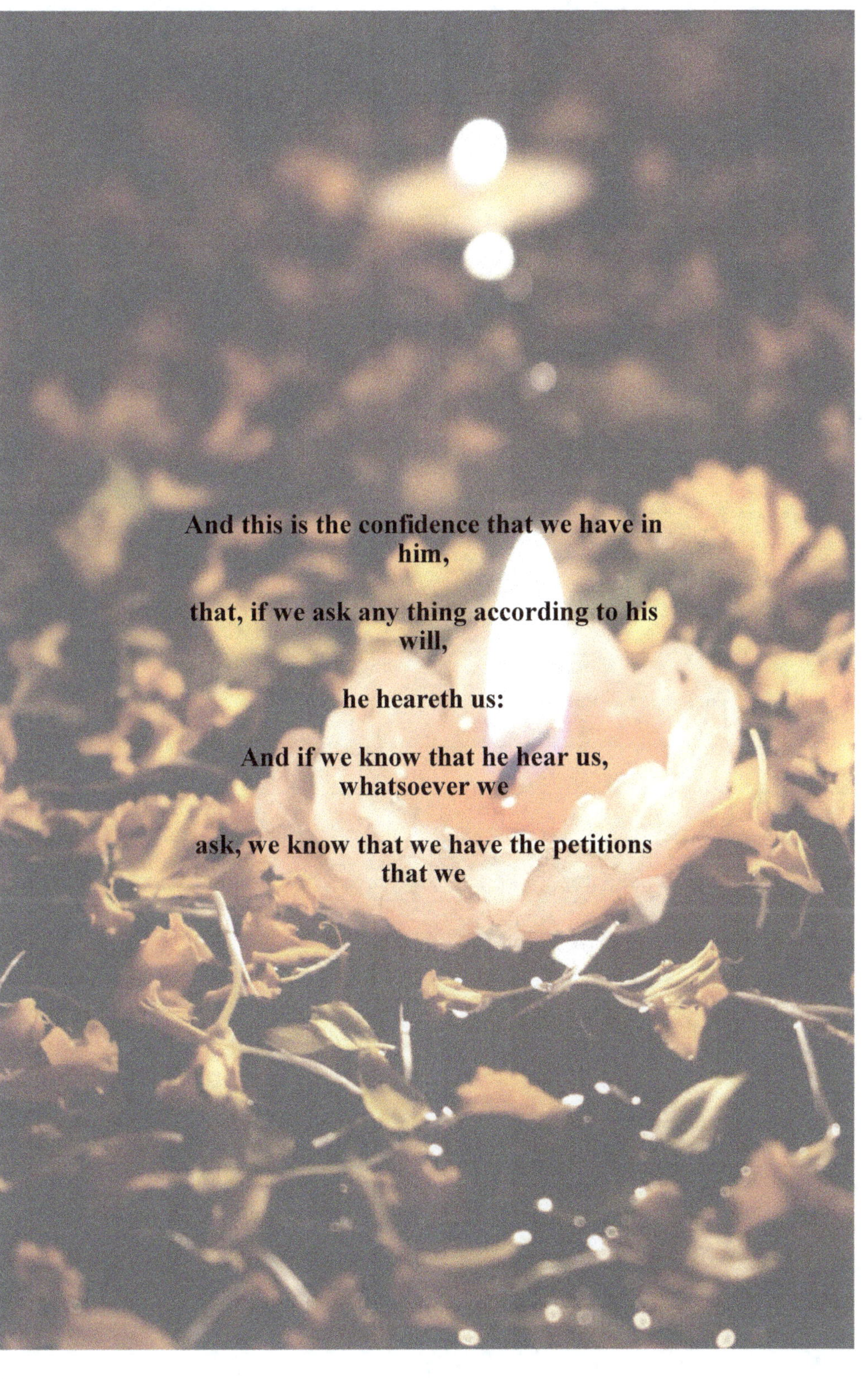
And this is the confidence that we have in him,
that, if we ask any thing according to his will,
he heareth us:
And if we know that he hear us, whatsoever we
ask, we know that we have the petitions that we

MY PRAYER JOURNAL

Thank You ______________________________

MY PRAYER JOURNAL

MY PRAYER JOURNAL

Thank You

MY PRAYER JOURNAL

MY PRAYER JOURNAL

Thank You

MY PRAYER JOURNAL

MY PRAYER JOURNAL

Thank You

MY PRAYER JOURNAL

MY PRAYER JOURNAL

Thank You

THANK YOU LORD

FOR

If ye abide in me, and my words abide in you, ye shall ask what ye will, and it shall be done unto you.

John 15:7

MY PRAYER JOURNAL

Thank You

MY PRAYER JOURNAL

MY PRAYER JOURNAL

Thank You

MY PRAYER JOURNAL

MY PRAYER JOURNAL

Thank You

MY PRAYER JOURNAL

MY PRAYER JOURNAL

Thank You

MY PRAYER JOURNAL

MY PRAYER JOURNAL

Thank You

THANK YOU LORD

FOR

The Lord is nigh unto all them that call upon him,

to all that call upon him in truth.

He will fulfil the desire of them that fear him: he

also will hear their cry, and will save them.

Psalm 145: 18-19

MY PRAYER JOURNAL

MY PRAYER JOURNAL

Thank You

MY PRAYER JOURNAL

MY PRAYER JOURNAL

Thank You

MY PRAYER JOURNAL

MY PRAYER JOURNAL

Thank You

MY PRAYER JOURNAL

MY PRAYER JOURNAL

Thank You

MY PRAYER JOURNAL

Thank You

THANK YOU LORD

FOR

Let us therefore come boldly unto the throne of
grace, that we may obtain mercy, and find grace
to help in time of need.
Hebrews 4:16

MY PRAYER JOURNAL

Thank You

MY PRAYER JOURNAL

MY PRAYER JOURNAL

Thank You

MY PRAYER JOURNAL

MY PRAYER JOURNAL

Thank You

MY PRAYER JOURNAL

Thank You

MY PRAYER JOURNAL

Thank You

THANK YOU LORD

FOR

And whatsoever we ask, we receive of him,
because we keep his commandments, and do
those things that are pleasing in his sight.
I John 3:22

MY PRAYER JOURNAL

Thank You

MY PRAYER JOURNAL

Thank You

If my people, which are called by my name,

shall humble themselves, and pray, and seek my

face, and turn from their wicked ways; then will

I hear from heaven, and will forgive their sin, and

will heal their land.

II Chronicles 7:14

MY PRAYER JOURNAL

MY PRAYER JOURNAL

Thank You

MY PRAYER JOURNAL

MY PRAYER JOURNAL

Thank You

MY PRAYER JOURNAL

Thank You

MY PRAYER JOURNAL

Thank You

MY PRAYER JOURNAL

MY PRAYER JOURNAL

Thank You

www.ingramcontent.com/pod-product-compliance
Lightning Source LLC
LaVergne TN
LVHW050538100826
845148LV00002B/599

* 9 7 8 1 7 3 7 9 9 1 4 2 7 *